CW00385903

TRAVELING THROUGH THE DARK

ALSO BY WILLIAM STAFFORD

# WILLIAM STAFFORD

# TRAVELING THROUGH

# THE DARK

WEATHER*light*
PRESS

TRAVELING THROUGH THE DARK
was first published in the United States of America
by Harper & Row in 1962

This first UK edition by Weatherlight Press ©1997
Published in co-operation with the Estate of William Stafford

Weatherlight Press
34 Cornwallis Crescent, Clifton
Bristol BS8 4PH

Designed by Ian Waddell
Printed by Aldgate Press

Distributed by Windhorse Publications
11 Park Road
Moseley
Birmingham B13 8AB
England

British Library Cataloguing in Publication Data
A Catalogue record for this book
is available from the British Library

ISBN 0-9522798-3-5

*Poems in this collection appeared in the following magazines:*
Approach, Beliot Poetry Journal, Botteghe Oscure, Colorado Quarterly, Contact,
December, Fiddlehead, Harper's Magazine, Hudson Review, Inland, Kenyon Review,
Listen, Nation, New Mexico Quarterly, New Orleans Poetry Journal, New Republic,
Northwest Review, Paris Review, Pioneer Log, Poetry, Poetry Book Society, Poetry
Northwest, Prairie Schooner, Saturday Review, Southwest Review, University of Portland
Review, Yale Review.

# Contents

*part one*

IN MEDIAS RES

# TRAVELING THROUGH THE DARK

Traveling through the dark I found a deer
dead on the edge of the Wilson River road.
It is usually best to roll them into the canyon:
that road is narrow; to swerve might make more dead.

By glow of the tail-light I stumbled back of the car
and stood by the heap, a doe, a recent killing;
she had stiffened already, almost cold.
I dragged her off; she was large in the belly.

My fingers touching her side brought me the reason—
her side was warm; her fawn lay there waiting,
alive, still, never to be born.
Beside that mountain road I hesitated.

The car aimed ahead its lowered parking lights;
under the hood purred the steady engine.
I stood in the glare of the warm exhaust turning red;
around our group I could hear the wilderness listen.

I thought hard for us all—my only swerving—,
then pushed her over the edge into the river.

# In Medias Res

On Main one night when they sounded the chimes
my father was ahead in shadow, my son,
behind coming into the streetlight, on each side
a brother and a sister; and overhead
the chimes went arching for the perfect sound.
There was a one-stride god on Main that night,
all walkers in a cloud.

I saw pictures, windows taking shoppers
where the city went, a great shield hammering out,
my wife loving the stations on that shield
and following into the shades calling back.
I had not thought to know the hero quite so well.
"Aeneas!" I cried, "just man, defender!"
And our town burned and burned.

# Elegy

The responsible sound of the lawnmower
puts a net under the afternoon;
closing the refrigerator door
I hear a voice in the other room
that starts up color in every cell:
> Presents like this, Father, I got from you,
> and there are hundreds more to tell.

One night, sound held in cornfield farms
drowned in August, and melonflower breath
creeping in stealth—we walked west
where all the rest of the country slept.
I hold that memory in both my arms—
> how the families there had starved the dogs;
> in the night they waited to be fed.

At the edge of dark there paled a flash—
a train came on with its soft tread
that roused itself with light and thundered
with dragged windows curving down earth's side
while the cornstalks whispered.
> All of us hungry creatures watched
> until it was extinguished.

If only once in all those years
the right goodbye could have been said!
I hear you climbing up the snow
a brown-clad wanderer on the road
with the usual crooked stick,
    and on the wrong side of the mountains
    I can hear the latches click.


Remember in the Southwest going down the canyons?
We turned off the engine, the tires went hoarse
picking up sound out of turned away mountains;
we felt the secret sky lean down.
Suddenly the car came to with a roar.
    And remember the Christmas wreath on our door—
    when we threw it away and it jumped blue up the fire?


At sight of angels or anything unusual
you are to mark the spot with a cross,
for I have set out to follow you
and these marked places are expected,
but in between I can hear no sound.
    The softest hush of doors I close
    may jump to slam in a March wind.

When you left our house that night and went falling
into that ocean, a message came: silence.
I pictured you going, spangles and bubbles
leaving your pockets in a wheel clockwise.
Sometimes I look out of our door at night.
When you send messages they come spinning
back into sound with just leaves rustling.

Come battering. I listen, am the same, waiting.

# A STARED STORY

Over the hill came horsemen, horsemen whistling.
They were all hard-driven, stamp, stamp, stamp.
Legs withdrawn and delivered again like pistons,
down they rode into the winter camp,
and while earth whirled on its forgotten center
those travelers feasted till dark in the lodge of their chief.
Into the night at last on earth their mother
they drummed away; the farthest hoofbeat ceased.

Often at cutbanks where roots hold dirt together
survivors pause in the sunlight, quiet, pretending
that stared story—and gazing at earth their mother:
all journey far, hearts beating, to some such ending.
And all, slung here in our cynical constellation,
whistle the wild world, live by imagination.

# Thinking for Berky

In the late night listening from bed
I have joined the ambulance or the patrol
screaming toward some drama, the kind of end
that Berky must have some day, if she isn't dead.

The wildest of all, her father and mother cruel,
farming out there beyond the old stone quarry
where highschool lovers parked their lurching cars,
Berky learned to love in that dark school.

Early her face was turned away from home
toward any hardworking place; but still her soul,
with terrible things to do, was alive, looking out
for the rescue that—surely, some day—would have to come.

Windiest nights, Berky, I have thought for you,
and no matter how lucky I've been I've touched wood.
There are things not solved in our town though tomorrow came:
there are things time passing can never make come true.

We live in an occupied country, misunderstood;
justice will take us millions of intricate moves.
Sirens will hunt down Berky, you survivors in your beds
listening through the night, so far and good.

# WITH MY CROWBAR KEY

I do tricks in order to know:
careless I dance,
then turn to see
the mark to turn God left for me.

Making my home in vertigo
I pray with my screams
and think with my hair
prehensile in the dark with fear.

When I hear the well bucket strike something soft
far down at noon,
then there's no place
far enough away to hide my face.

When I see my town over sights of a rifle,
and carved by light
from the lowering sun,
then my old friends darken one by one.

By step and step like a cat toward God
I dedicated walk,
but under the house
I realize the kitten's crouch.

And by night like this I turn and come
to this possible house
which I open, and see
myself at work with this crowbar key.

# THE THOUGHT MACHINE

Its little eye stares "On" in its forehead
by its maker's name. They say it anticipates
its memories and holds "Eureka!" tight
in little wheels so sure that all steel
hardens when incorporated in it.
The only Please it knows is, Be Correct;
but it can tolerate mistakes.

You tell your troubles to it, how your letters
all came back with no acknowledgement
and all you wanted was assurance all was known.
It tugs its collar; its little eye glows on.
You tell about the woman at the corner
ringing the bell to bring Jesus and his weather.
That is long ago.

You tell of the hill that never attracted the deer;
you think it frightened them, a fear place,
where you always had to go to listen—it was
for your town and for the world; it was for . . . —
and you are back there, listening again:
the little eye goes kind; the forehead
has the noble look that hill had.

And the world whirls into vision; in Tibet
a prayer wheel turns for you; an Eskimo
by such a northern fire lives that you live so,
touching only important things;
you see that all machines belong;
the deer are safe;
a letter has reached home.

# MOUSE NIGHT: ONE OF OUR GAMES

We heard thunder. Nothing great—on high
ground rain began. Who ran through
that rain? I shrank, a fieldmouse, when
the thunder came—under grass with bombs
of water scything stems. My tremendous
father cowered: "Lions rushing make
that sound," he said; "we'll be brain-washed
for sure if head-size chunks of water hit us.
Duck and cover! It takes a man
to be a mouse this night," he said.

# PARENTAGE

My father didn't really belong in history.
He kept looking over his shoulder at some mistake.
He was a stranger to me, for I belong.

There never was a particular he couldn't understand,
but there were too many in too long a row,
and like many another he was overwhelmed.

Today drinking coffee I look over the cup
and want to have the right amount of fear,
preferring to be saved and not, like him, heroic.

I want to be as afraid as the teeth are big,
I want to be as dumb as the wise are wrong:
I'd just as soon be pushed by events to where I belong.

# The Research Team in the Mountains

We have found a certain heavy kind of wolf.
Haven't seen it, though —
just *know* it.

Answers are just echoes, they say. But
a question travels before it comes back,
and that counts.

Did you know that here everything is free?
We've found days that wouldn't allow a price
on anything.

When a dirty river and a clean river
come together the result is —
dirty river.

If your policy is to be friends in the mountains
a rock falls on you: the only real friends —
you can't help it.

Many go home having "conquered a mountain" —
they leave their names at the top in a jar
for snow to remember.

Looking out over the campfire at night
again this year I pick a storm for you,
again the first one.

We climbed Lostine and Hurricane and Chief Joseph canyons;
finally in every canyon the road ends.
Above that—storms of stone.

# Holding the Sky

We saw a town by the track in Colorado.
Cedar trees below had sifted the air,
snow water foamed the torn river there,
and a lost road went climbing the slope like a ladder.

We were traveling between a mountain and Thursday,
holding pages back on the calendar,
remembering every turn in the roadway:
we could hold that sky, we said, and remember.

On the western slope we crashed into Thursday.
"So long," you said when the train stopped there.
Snow was falling, touching in the air.
Those dark mountains have never wavered.

# THE JOB

It starts before light—
all that story of the stars,
night winking meaning,
dawn still frozen, and in dark spells
in our little town, at zero in winter,
from every house plumed furnaces announcing themselves;
from our house a great gray promise
promising upward and out from town: dawn.

We feel confident.
Into some local brain we think the story will come
like swallows into a house, anyone's head, any thought's home.
The church rises from its trees and holds
its true darkness tall, nearly visible,
then really tall till the earth rings; the bells
only swing in the cold silently opening
their mouths; and we walk into the call of the college.

Now the hall takes us toward quiet,
past the stairwell where Foucault's pendulum
remembers how the earth used to spin;
we turn again, enter the classroom,
look at the deep faces looking at us,
deep in our school, waiting under the school roof;
we open the book with care and hold our breath:
begin—translating the vast versions of the wind.

# PRAIRIE TOWN

There was a river under First and Main;
the salt mines honeycombed farther down.
A wealth of sun and wind ever so strong
converged on that home town, long gone.

At the north edge there were the sandhills.
I used to stare for hours at prairie dogs,
which had their town, and folded their little paws
to stare beyond their fence where I was.

River rolling in secret, salt mines with care
holding your crystals and stillness, north prairie—
what kind of trip can I make, with what old friend,
ever to find a town so widely rich again?

Pioneers, for whom history was walking through dead grass,
and the main things that happened were miles and the time of day—
you built that town, and I have let it pass.
Little folded paws, judge me: I came away.

# TORNADO

First the soul of our house left, up the chimney,
and part of the front window went outward—pursued
whatever tore at the chest. Part of the lake
on top guyed around the point, bellied
like a tent; and fish like seeds ripened felt
a noiseless Command around their gills, while
the wheatfields crouched, reminded with a hand.

That treble talk always at the bottom of the creek
at the mouth, where the lake leaned away from the rock
at the mouth, rose above water. Then Command moved
away again and our town spread, ruined
but relieved, at the bottom of its remembered air.
We weren't left religion exactly (the church
was ecumenical bricks), but a certain tall element:
a pulse beat still in the stilled rock
and in the buried sound along the buried mouth of the creek.

# CONSERVATIVE

Indiana felt the ice,
yet holds wide lakes against that pain:
I lived in Indiana once,
put these hands into those lakes
of counties near Fort Wayne.

You come a river, then our town
where summer domes the elms that hide
the river, which—a lurking home—
reflects in windows all the clouds
that drift that countryside.

All you that live your city way:
you cannot hold thought ways to hold
the old way steady; nowadays
you cannot hear the songs we sang
or know what glaciers told,

So I'll say this, then stand apart,
allegiant to where we lived
all the way to cross my heart:
*Your years—these riffles atoms made—*
*and your map river-carved*

*Conceal a map new glaciers plan;*
*and there are rivers yet to come,*
*wide lakes again, and maybe hands*
*to dip like mine; a voice to say:*
"For towns, I'll take this one."

# THE WOMAN AT BANFF

While she was talking a bear happened along, violating
every garbage can. Shaking its loose, Churchillian,
V for victory suit, it ripped up and ate
a greasy "Bears Are Dangerous!" sign.

While she was talking the trees above signalled—
"Few," and the rock back of them—"Cold."
And while she was talking a moose—huge, black—
swam that river and faded off winterward,

Up toward the Saskatchewan.

# THE TILLAMOOK BURN

These mountains have heard God;
they burned for weeks. He spoke
in a tongue of flame from sawmill trash
and you can read His word down to the rock.

In milky rivers the steelhead
butt upstream to spawn
and find a world with depth again,
starting from stillness and water across gray stone.

Inland along the canyons
all night weather smokes
past the deer and the widow-makers—
trees too dead to fall till again He speaks,

Mowing the criss-cross trees and the listening peaks.

# THE OLD HAMER PLACE

The wind came every night like an animal
rushing our house, disappearing before day,
leaving us all we could stand of the way it would be
when a hand always raised over the world fell,
or when horizontal tomorrow dimensioned out
from a scene so deep it captured our eyes.
    The animal made off thrashing limbs,
    taking a message in its heavy shoulders
    into the lean hills among the low stars, crashing.

All this had got lost from my mind: now
no one in all the world tonight is
even thinking about that hollow house
when the truck left years ago and the moaning
seasons began to wander through the room, stirring
vines and their shadows that grew in the dark.
    I touch that wall, collapsing it there where
    no one knows, by the quivering owl sound
    in a forest no one knows.

But the world is loaded with places for tomorrow to visit,
though this had got lost from my mind,
how the truck left years ago.
Enough air moves any morning for stillness to
come where the windows are. A place that
changed is a different place, but
    *A whole town might come shuddering back, that had disappeared*
    *when a dark animal began to overcome the world*
    *and a little bird came to sing our walls down.*

# On Quitting a Little College

By footworn boards, by steps
that sagged years after the pride of workmen,
by things that had to *do* so long they now seemed right,
by ways of acting so old they grooved the people
(and all this among fields that never quit
under a patient sky),
I taught. And then I quit.

"Let's walk home," the president said.
He faced down the street,
and on the rollers of bird flight
through the year-round air
that little town became all it had promised him.
He could not quit; he could not let go fast enough;
his duties carried him.

The bitter habit of the forlorn cause
is my addiction. I miss it now, but face
ahead and go in my own way
toward my own place.

# Reporting Back

By the secret that holds the forest up,
no one will escape. (We have reached this place.)

The sky will come home some day.
(We pay all mistakes our bodies make when they move.)

Is there a way to walk that living has obscured?
(Our feet are trying to remember some path we are walking
toward.)

# The Poets' Annual Indigence Report

Tonight beyond the determined moon,
aloft with nothing left that is voluntary
for delight, everything uttering hydrogen,
your thinkers are mincing along through a hail of contingencies,

While we all—floating though we are, lonesome though we are,
lost in hydrogen—we live by seems things:
when things just *are*, then something else
will be doing the living.

Doing is not enough; being is not enough;
knowing is far from enough. So we clump around, putting
feet on the dazzle floor, awaiting the real schedule
by celebrating the dazzle schedule.

And, whatever is happening, we are here;
a lurch or a god has brought us together.
We do our jobs—listening in fear
in endless, friendless, Jesus-may-happen fashion.

Our shadows ride over the grass, your shadows, ours:—
Rich men, wise men, be our contemporaries.

# In Response to a Question

The earth says have a place, be what that place
requires; hear the sound the birds imply
and see as deep as ridges go behind
each other. (Some people call their scenery flat,
their only picture framed by what they know:
I think around them rise a riches and a loss
too equal for their chart—but absolutely tall.)

The earth says every summer have a ranch
that's minimum: one tree, one well, a landscape
that proclaims a universe—sermon
of the hills, hallelujah mountain,
highway guided by the way the world is tilted,
reduplication of mirage, flat evening:
a kind of ritual for the wavering.

The earth says where you live wear the kind
of color that your life is (gray shirt for me)
and by listening with the same bowed head that sings
draw all into one song, join
the sparrow on the lawn, and row that easy
way, the rage without met by the wings
within that guide you anywhere the wind blows.

Listening, I think that's what the earth says.

# WITH ONE LAUNCHED LOOK

The cheetah levels at one far deer
rejecting all others in his charge,
connecting toward the chosen throat
—a dedicated follower.

It is that choice that quells the deer,
such a fateful diagram:
bisecting all the irrelevant world
—one launched look and its afterward.

## B.C.

The seed that met water spoke a little name.

(Great sunflowers were lording the air that day;
this was before Jesus, before Rome; that other air
was readying our hundreds of years to say things
that rain has beat down on over broken stones
and heaped behind us in many slag lands.)

Quiet in the earth a drop of water came,
and the little seed spoke: "Sequoia is my name."

# CAPTIVE

Calmly through the bars observe
how correct a tiger is:
the striped fur blends with cages;
how the iron parallels
the paw freed by your—calmly!—eye;
and if it's a big one—coincide—
how the stripes become the bars:
tiger flesh rejoins a fawn's,
commitment to the cub he was
before a shadow caged his ribs;
how he glides by appropriateness
into jungles while you stand
outside his eyes, beyond his bars:
captor, witness, victim—calmed.

# THE VIEW FROM HERE

In Antarctica drooping their little shoulders
like bottles the penguins stand, small,
sad, black—and the wind
bites hard over them.

Edging that continent they huddle to turn their eyes.
Penguins, we can't help you; and all that cold
hangs over us too, wide beyond thought.
We too stand and wait.

## LIT INSTRUCTOR

Day after day up there beating my wings
with all of the softness truth requires
I feel them shrug whenever I pause:
they class my voice among tentative things,

And they credit fact, force, battering.
I dance my way toward the family of knowing,
embracing stray error as a long-lost boy
and bringing him home with my fluttering.

Every quick feather asserts a just claim;
it bites like a saw into white pine.
I communicate right; but explain to the dean—
well, Right has a long and intricate name.

And the saying of it is a lonely thing.

# THE STAR IN THE HILLS

A star hit in the hills behind our house
up where the grass turns brown touching the sky.

Meteors have hit the world before, but this was near,
and since TV; few saw, but many felt the shock.
The state of California owns that land
(and out from shore three miles), and any stars
that come will be roped off and viewed on week days 8 to 5.

A guard who took the oath of loyalty and denied
any police record told me this:
"If you don't have a police record yet
you could take the oath and get a job
if California should be hit by another star."

"I'd promise to be loyal to California
and to guard any stars that hit it," I said,
"or any place three miles out from shore,
unless the star was bigger than the state—
in which case I'd be loyal to *it*."

But he said no exceptions were allowed,
and he leaned against the state-owned meteor
so calm and puffed a cork-tip cigarette
that I looked down and traced with my foot in the dust
and thought again and said, "Ok—any star."

# I Was in the City All Day

Into the desert, trading people for horses,
the leader rode toward a responsible act:
the having one person at the last campfire,
telling just the next thing to that one person,
with all around only the waiting night waiting,
in the shadows horses eating wild hay—
and then the last word without distraction,
one meaning like a bird slipping out into the dark.

# A Poet to a Novelist

When we write, fighting feedback, eedback, dback,
back, ack of the forward part of our brains,
a perfect flower blooms from all failure; we hear
every wrong number down a tincan telephone line jangle the
    bells
till the neighbors' ears are supporting the line,
everybody's effort scaled down, aled down, d down, down
toward disappearing—all who lunge plunging.
We let them go by at the world's pace.

There are hills our windows give every winter;
when we close the curtains we know the streetlight is left
outside alone; from the end of the street (this is the edge of
    town)
the few slant flakes come out of the dark and fall on the house
that goes deaf while night fans over the roof.
Such arrivals in storms are one kind of chance,
a difference we want after our days doing
one thing at a time, the way purpose is.

We take everything stacked, being all at once
like a jewel and then into some act; we pass calendar knots
through our hands, remembering not just important things—
maybe the welcome a Western town gave early women,
dust from the alley past the clothesline, anybody's sky
sighting down given streets, years like a fan opening
and then closing. We pay it out (still owing what's near us
every aid, no matter the worth, because it is near).

We hear such blossom syllables in the sounds that rise
that we cannot find a path among true words,
redundant honesty of the scrupulous; we go down
with what occurs to any length, echoes realer
than originals, coming from cliffs the air belongs on
or comes back to sideways. We happen in the night
on orchards that stutter whiteness as the moon passes:
spring comes every night when luck is there.

We owe the twilight aid because day
once prevailed: the bad parts run a world
ready to fade but still present if a person
will come out from his eyes and be willing to hold
what he views. We welcome all back the child's way—
the finding of new things or sorting through gravel
or discovering the scent of alfalfa
that knows water out of the desert in the evening.

Over the night arc our need reaches for duty,
our state a glimmer to be good. Putting down
the last book or finding the light on the wall
by feel and memory, we veer toward the saintly,
say "Sorry!" (But we rebel at only the good:—
read and do what you want, and don't even be eager
to find the best—no finicky appetites.) No place
is wide enough to be sorry in, not any place.

Because you walk for us, we call you this,
"pilgrim for rain." No one else will meet us
low enough to hear wind in the grass
and let it go over our place. We wait,
low and looking for the oat spire against the sun,
leaf and straw, hay attached by accident to the ground.
Because we write we know the cost
of every day—the cost is all the rest.

Because you know it so, I give you this.

## UNIVERSE IS ONE PLACE

Crisis they call it?—when
when the gentle wheat leans at the combine and
and the farm girl brings cool jugs wrapped in burlap
slapping at her legs?

We think—drinking cold water
water looking at the sky—
*Sky is home, universe is one place.*
Crisis? City folks make

Make such a stir.
Farm girl away through the wheat.

# In the Night Desert

The Apache word for love twists
    then numbs the tongue:
Uttered once clear, said—
    never that word again.

"Cousin," you call, or "Sister" and one
    more word that spins
In the dust: a talk-flake
    chipped like obsidian.

The girl who hears this flake and
    follows you into the dark
Turns at a touch: the night desert
    forever behind her back.

*part two*

BEFORE THE BIG STORM

# Before the Big Storm

You are famous in my mind.
When anyone mentions your name
all the boxes marked "1930's"
fall off the shelves;
and the orators on the Fourth of July
all begin shouting again.
The audience of our high school commencement
begin to look out of the windows at the big storm.

And I think of you in our play—
oh, helpless and lonely!—crying,
and your father is dead again.
He was drunk; he fell.

When they mention your name,
our houses out there in the wind
creak again in the storm;
and I lean from our play, wherever I am,
to you, quiet at the edge of that town:
"All the world is blowing away."
"It is almost daylight."
"Are you warm?"

# THINGS WE DID THAT MEANT SOMETHING

Thin as memory to a bloodhound's nose,
being the edge of some new knowing,
I often glance at a winter color—
husk or stalk, a sunlight touch,
maybe a wasp nest in the brush
near the winter river with silt like silver.

Once with a slingshot I hit a wasp nest:—
without direction but sure of right,
released from belief and into act,
hornets planed off by their sincere faith.
Vehement response for them was enough,
patrolling my head with its thought like a moth:—

"Sometime the world may be hit like this
or I getting lost may walk toward this color
far in old sunlight with no trace at all,
till only the grass will know I fall."

# At Liberty School

Girl in the front row who had no mother
and went home every day to get supper,
the class became silent when you left early.

Elaborate histories were in our book
but of all the races you were the good:
the taxes of Rome were at your feet.

When the bell rang we did not write anymore.
Traitor to everything else, we poured
to the fountain. I bent and thought of you.

Our town now is Atlantis, crystal-water-bound;
at the door of the schoolhouse fish are swimming round;
thinking in and out of the church tower go deep waves.

Girl in the front row who had no mother,
as I passed the alleys of our town toward supper
there were not spiteful nails in any board.

# LAKE CHELAN

They call it regional, this relevance—
the deepest place we have: in this pool forms
the model of our land, a lonely one,
responsive to the wind. Everything we own
has brought us here: from here we speak.

The sun stalks among these peaks to sight
the lake down aisles, long like a gun;
a ferryboat, lost by a century, toots
for trappers, the pelt of the mountains
rinsed in the sun and that sound.

Suppose a person far off to whom this lake
occurs: told a problem, he might hear a word
so dark he drowns an instant, and stands dumb
for the centuries of his country and the suave
hills beyond the stranger's sight.

Is this man dumb, then, for whom Chelan lives
in the wilderness? On the street you've seen
someone like a trapper's child pause,
and fill his eyes with some irrelevant flood—
a tide stops him, delayed in his job.

Permissive as a beach, he turns inland,
harks like a fire, glances through the dark
like an animal drinking, and arrives along that line
a lake has found far back in the hills
where what comes finds a brim gravity exactly requires.

# THE MUSEUM AT TILLAMOOK

Still faces on the wall: that look
the early camera gave—hold still for time.
We walk down the corridor, looking history
back and forth: spearheads in one room,
bombs and pictures of our Navy blimp
in another, one hundred years between.

Joe Champion: first white settler,
hater of statistics, non-average.
(Indian Adams gave relics for the story.)
Joe carved this thing to eat with—a spoon,
sort of; he made this cradle for a baby
and this other kind of cradle, for grain.

Here is the hollow tree Joe inhabited—
his house, at first, before he taught
and prospered and died.
(Sold 500 acres for $400—got rich that way.)
Where's his grave?

This dugout—canoe or coffin—came down the flood
in 1949, buried six feet deep in the Nehalem Spit.
There's "The Morning Star," all sails spread,
near the twins, age 84.
One of them—older looking—saw something
above the camera: the eyes go back. . . .

Upstairs other creatures from the wild
have gathered—cold, natural scenes: an owl of snow,
a wolf with clear eyes looking down over the blown
bird's eggs, through the floor
past The Morning Star
into Joe's hollow tree.

# LATE AT NIGHT

Falling separate into the dark
the hailstone yelps of geese pattered
through our roof; startled we listened.

Those V's of direction swept by unseen
so orderly that we paused. But then
faltering back through their circle they came.

Were they lost up there in the night?
They always knew the way, we thought.
You looked at me across the room:—

We live in a terrible season.

# SUMMER WILL RISE

Summer will rise till the houses fear;
streets will hear underground streams;
purple, the banished color, will flare.
*This is the town where the vine will come.*

People will listen but will not hear.
Eyes will wizen to find a friend.
When no one is watching the candleflame
*this is the town where the wind will come.*

The trees will hear, farther than winter,
over the town a coming of birds.
What great wild hands will reach for them?
*—and for all who are here when those wanderers come?*

# FALL JOURNEY

Evening came, a paw, to the gray hut by the river.
Pushing the door with a stick, I opened it.
Only a long walk had brought me there,
steps into the continent they had placed before me.

I read weathered log, stone fireplace, broken chair,
the dead grass outside under the cottonwood tree—
and it all stared back. We've met before, my memory
started to say, somewhere. . . .

And then I stopped: my father's eyes were gray.

# A DEDICATION

We stood by the library. It was an August night.
Priests and sisters of hundreds of unsaid creeds
passed us going their separate pondered roads.
We watched them cross under the corner light.

Freights on the edge of town were carrying away
flatcars of steel to be made into secret guns;
we knew, being human, that they were enemy guns,
and we were somehow vowed to poverty.

No one stopped or looked long or held out a hand.
They were following orders received from hour to hour,
so many signals, all strange, from a foreign power:
*But tomorrow,* you whispered, *peace may flow over the land.*

At that corner in a flash of lightning we two stood;
that glimpse we had will stare through the dark forever:
on the poorest roads we would be walkers and beggars,
toward some deathless meeting involving a crust of bread.

## CHICKENS THE WEASEL KILLED

A passerby being fair about sacrifice,
with no program but walking,
no acrobat of salvation,
I couldn't help seeing the weasel
fasten on the throat.

Any vision isolates:
those chickens the weasel killed—
I hear them relax years from now,
subsiding while they threaten,
and then appeal to the ground with their wings.

# REQUIEM

Mother is gone. Bird songs wouldn't let her breathe.
The skating bug broke through the eternal veil.
A tree in the forest fell; the air remembered.
Two rocks clinked in the night to signal some meaning.

Traveler north, beyond where you can return,
hearing above you the last of the razor birds whizz
over the drift of dust that bore your name,
there's a kind of waiting you teach us—the art of not knowing.

Suicidal gestures of nobility driven to the wrist,
our molten bodies remembering some easier form,
we feel the bones assert the rites of yesterday
and the flow of angular events becoming destiny.

Summer and locusts own the elm part of town;
on the millpond moss is making its cream.
Our duty is just a certain high kind of waiting;
beyond our hearing is the hearing of the community.

# THE LAST FRIEND

In every life poor body earns its own evil,
some promised blow or sickness that will be final;
hungrily searching, poor body gets killed.

A long romance curves down towards that marriage—
a radiant virus, a processional fever.
Hear the peals of reunion in the broken-hearted aged!

Somewhere in a hall, hear the bride hurry
toward a meeting of rapture to which all are bidden—
poor body, poor lover, in one grave buried.

## "The Lyf So Short..."

We have lived in that room larger than the world,
cage in gold, corona in the dark,
where Chaucer let the pen go its quiet work
netting Criseyde, weeping as he wrote.

That man in the monk's hood climbs through flower stems
looking up at us his condemned man's look:
on secret pilings an imagined tide goes out,
over the sky go padding feet,

While we are forced backward into our dreams.
We are all sons of medieval kings;
"O alma redemptoris" is a grain on our tongue,
but no saint's hand can pluck the pain from us:—

Today we have to stand in absolute rain
and face whatever comes from God,
or stoop to smooth the earth over little things
that went into dirt, out of the world.

# The Only Card I got on My Birthday
## Was from an Insurance Man

On upland farms into abandoned wells
on a line meridian high
state by state my birthday star comes on
and peers, my birthday night,
and in my eyes it stands while past its light
the world and I turn, just and far, till
every well scans over the year like spokes
of a wheel returning the long soft look of the sky.

Star in a well, dark message: when I die,
my glance drawn over galaxies,
all through one night let a candle nurse the dark
to mark this instant of what I was,
this once—not putting my hand out
blessing for business' sake any frail markers
of human years: we want real friends or none;
what's genuine will accompany every man.

Who travel these lonely wells can drink that star.

# AT THE OLD PLACE

The beak of dawn's rooster pecked
in the sky, and early Ella
called us.
I awoke to worse than sleep,
and saw things clear beyond the barn,
and Ella older.

That was years—barns—ago.
But should another rooster crow
I'd be more wise,
listen better in the dawn,
wake at once to more than day—
to Ella always.

# LOVE THE BUTCHER BIRD LURKS
# EVERYWHERE

A gather of apricots fruit pickers left
gleam like reasons for light going higher, higher;
I look half as hard as I can to tease
the fruit out of its green.
    (It is time to run lest pity overtake us,
    and calamity pity invents to accompany itself:
    to sigh is a stern act—we are judged by this air.)


Down the steady eye of the charging bear
a gun barrel swerves—intention, then flame;
and willows do tricks to find an exact place in the wind:
resolution steady, bent to be true.
    (While there's time
    I call to you by all these dubious guides:
    "Forsake all ways except the way we came.")

## LEARNING

A needle knows everything lengthwise
enforcing only the least radius
being hardly meant at all,
  single, straight, serious.
     But it is late, it is always late.

If I knew enough it would all be gradual,
every departure, every arrival,
small radius, in, out, returning,
like the needle's eye always learning.
     But it is late, it is always late.

Worlds can swerve while I stammer;
the stars come different at night and nearer.
I can't learn even how to enter
what awaits me every year.

     And it is late, I know it.

## ADULTS ONLY

Animals own a fur world;
people own worlds that are variously, pleasingly, bare.
And the way these worlds *are* once arrived for us kids
        with a jolt,
that night when the wild woman danced
in the giant cage we found we were all in
at the state fair.

Better women exist, no doubt, than that one,
and occasions more edifying, too, I suppose.
But we have to witness for ourselves what comes
        for us,
nor be distracted by barkers of irrelevant ware;
and a pretty good world, I say, arrived that night
when that woman came farming right out of her clothes,
by God,

At the state fair.

# WISTERIA JONES

She used to write, ribboning our talk away,
turning it onto itself many layers
and steeping the prose hills into purple highlands,
merely by distancing.

"Purple is the realest thing about the hills,"
she used to say—
"it's where we used to stand."
If I met her today I'd say that now.

# IN THE MUSEUM

Like that, I put the next thing in your hand—
this piece of rock the farthest climbers found,
or this, a broken urn volcano-finished.

Later you'll walk out and say, "Where's home?"
There will be something lacking in each room,
a part you held and casually laid down.

You never can get back, but there'll be other
talismans. You have learned to falter
in this good way: stand still, walk on, remember—

Let one by one things come alive like fish
and swim away into their future waves.

# TIME'S EXILE

From all encounters vintages ensue,
bitter, flat, or redolent. When we met
sunflowers were in bloom.
They mark the highway into Kansas yet.

My unreal errands, once the sun goes down,
fade into streetlight shadows.
Extenuate as the bright lights will, they run
into the hometown shadows.

I'm alongside old happenings when they flare;
like the dog that found the wounded quail
that came up through breast-feather shadows
into the sights and set their wings and sailed

The proximate field, and melted with shot
into another field—I bring things back from everywhere.
I am a man who detours through the park,
a man like those we used to meet back there—

Whose father had a son,
who has a son,
who finds his way by sunflowers through the dark.

# BIRTHDAY

We have a dog named "Here";
the tame half wags; the bitter
half will freeze, paw still,
and look at the place the world came from.
I have explored Here's shoulder,
patting it. There is a muscle there
that levels mountains, or forbids.

The weather is telling Here a north story:
someone is lost in a waver of peaks in snow,
and only he gets the signal, tired;
has to turn north, even to teeth of the wind—
that is the only road to go,
through storm dark, by seams in the rock, peering.
Someone is always calling out in the snow.

Here stands by me. I am forty-five,
deep in a story strongly told. I've turned;
I know I will again— a straightness
never quite attained. The curve I try
to find becomes a late intention.
I pat Here's shoulder sometimes,
and we watch the clear sky bend.

## GLANCES

Two people meet. The sky turns winter,
quells whatever they would say.
Then, a periphery glance into danger—
and an avalanche already on its way.

They have been honest all of their lives;
careful, calm, never in haste;
they didn't know what it is to *meet*.
Now they have met: the world is waste.

They find they are riding an avalanche
feeling at rest, all danger gone.
The present looks out of their eyes; they stand
calm and still on a speeding stone.

# FALL WIND

Pods of summer crowd around the door;
I take them in the autumn of my hands.

Last night I heard the first cold wind outside;
the wind blew soft, and yet I shiver twice:

Once for thin walls, once for the sound of time.

# A Pippa Lilted

Good things will happen
when the green flame of spring
goes up into hills where
we'd have our ranch if
we had the money.

It will be soon—
we'll hold our arms ready,
long toward the table
like Cézanne's people,
and let the light pour.

Just wait a little more—
let new errors cancel
the things we did wrong.
That's the right way for us:
our errors will dance.

It will be soon;
good things will happen.

# THE TRIP

Our car was fierce enough;
no one could tell we were only ourselves;
so we drove, equals of the car,
and ate at a drive-in where Citizens were dining.
A waitress with eyes made up to be Eyes
brought food spiced by the neon light.

Watching, we saw the manager greet people—
hollow on the outside, some kind of solid veneer.
When we got back on the road we welcomed
it as a fierce thing welcomes the cold.
Some people you meet are so dull
that you always remember their names.

*part three*

REPRESENTING FAR PLACES

# REPRESENTING FAR PLACES

In the canoe wilderness branches wait for winter;
every leaf concentrates; a drop from the paddle falls.
Up through water at the dip of a falling leaf
to the sky's drop of light or the smell of another star
fish in the lake leap arcs of realization,
hard fins prying out from the dark below.

Often in society when the talk turns witty
you think of that place, and can't polarize at all:
it would be a kind of treason. The land fans in your head
canyon by canyon; steep roads diverge.
Representing far places you stand in the room,
all that you know merely a weight in the weather.

It is all right to be simply the way you have to be,
among contradictory ridges in some crescendo of knowing.

# FROM THE GRADUAL GRASS

Imagine a voice calling,
"There is a voice now calling,"
or maybe a blasting cry:
"Walls are falling!"
as it makes walls be falling.

Then from the gradual grass,
too serious to be only noise—
whatever it is grass makes,
making words, a voice:
"Destruction is ending; this voice

"Is promising quiet: silence
by lasting forever grows to sound
endlessly from the world's end
promising, calling."
Imagine. *That voice is calling.*

# LONG DISTANCE

Sometimes when you watch the fire
ashes glow and gray
the way the sun turned cold on spires
in winter in the town back home
so far away.

Sometimes on the telephone
the one you hear goes far
and ghostly voices whisper in.
You think they are from other wires.
You think they are.

# The Peters Family

At the end of their ragged field
a new field began:
miles told the sunset that Kansas
would hardly ever end,
and that beyond the Cimarron crossing
and after the row-crop land
a lake would surprise the country
and sag with a million birds.

You couldn't analyze those people—
a no-pattern had happened to them:
their field opened and opened,
level, and more, then forever,
never crossed. Their world went everywhere.

# In Fear and Valor

My mother was afraid
and in my life her fear has hid:
when Perseus holds the Gorgon's head
she cringes, naked.

Clothed in my body, wild,
even as I grew strong,
my mother, weeping, suffered
the whole world's wrong.

Vanquished and trembling before she died,
she claimed a place in every limb:
my mother, lost in my stride, fears Death,
as I hunt him.

# THE TITLE COMES LATER

In my sleep a little man cries, "Faker! Faker!"
and I tell myself mildly and seriously
    that it is well to listen;
but in sleep it is that I evade: awake,
I meet the whole weather of my life,
    cold and real.
(The title is "Remembering, or
Guide Your Dreams Awake.")

In sleep all dreams belong, correcting each other;
but in blizzards of our waking all possible worlds
    are fighting each other.
"Every act in every dream deserves to live,"
I tell myself, mildly and seriously:
    "accept the law that grounds your being;
awake, asleep, or neither, everything belongs."
But awaking from awaking, I am a little man myself crying,
    "Faker! Faker!"

# AT COVE ON THE CROOKED RIVER

At Cove at our camp in the open canyon
it was the kind of place where you might look out
some evening and see trouble walking away.

And the river there meant something
always coming from snow and flashing around boulders
after shadow-fish lurking below the mesa.

We stood with wet towels over our heads for shade,
looking past the Indian picture rock and the kind of trees
that act out whatever has happened to them.

Oh civilization, I want to carve you like this,
decisively outward the way evening comes
over that kind of twist in the scenery

When people cramp into their station wagons
and roll up the windows, and drive away.

# LAST VACATION

Mountains crowded around on the north.
Hoisting our cage we went walk, walk.
Where, however, was home?
Tired, we set our cage down.

A zebra view. The black we could see through,
past that other, past its fire;
we could look out far through the black.
But glowing between lay the bars world:

Like an old house where our hearts had beat,
like a window burning at the end of our street.
The calendar fell for thirty days
like a bent jail sky over two meteors.

# LOOKING FOR SOMEONE

### 1

Many a time driving over the Coast Range,
down the cool side—hemlock, spruce, then shore pine—
I've known something I should have said one time:
"If we hadn't met, then everything would have to change."

### 2

We were judged; our shadows knew our height,
and after dark, exact, the air confirmed
all with its move or stillness:
we both were trapped on an odd-shaped island.

### 3

Sleet persuades a traveler: I all night
know no under the earth escape
even when the sky goes back remote.
Walking till the stars forget, I look out

### 4

And watch the smoke at Astoria and Seaside
cringing along the coast, and barefoot gulls
designing the sand: "Go flat, go flat,"—the waves;
the little boat, the mild riding light,

5

The sand going democratic, trading places down the wind,
everything distancing away. Finding this
took all this time, and you're not even here.
Though we met, everything had to change.

# WHAT GOD USED FOR EYES
## BEFORE WE CAME

At night sometimes the big fog roams in tall
from the coast and away tall on the mountain road
it stands without moving while cars wander along
in the canyons they make with their lights maintaining
    the worth
of local things. Along the continent shelf and back
far for searching the light engages the stone.

The brain blurring to know wanders that road,
goes the way Jesus came, irresistible,
calm over irrelevant history
toward a continent wall that moth rays touch—
our land backed by being old at night, lying deep,
the gray air holding ruin rock at Hovenweep.

# RETURNED TO SAY

When I face north a lost Cree
on some new shore puts a moccasin down,
rock in the light and noon for seeing,
he in a hurry and I beside him.

It will be a long trip; he will be a new chief;
we have drunk new water from an unnamed stream;
under little dark trees he is to find a path
we both must travel because we have met.

Henceforth we gesture even by waiting;
there is a grain of sand on his knifeblade
so small he blows it and while his breathing
darkens the steel his eyes become set

And start a new vision: the rest of his life.
We will mean what he does. Back of this page
the path turns north. We are looking for a sign.
Our moccasins do not mark the ground.

# FOUND IN A STORM

A storm that needed a mountain
met it where we were:
we woke up in a gale
that was reasoning with our tent,
and all the persuaded snow
streaked along, guessing the ground.

We turned from that curtain, down.
But sometime we will turn
back to the curtain and go
by plan through an unplanned storm,
disappearing into the cold,
meanings in search of a world.

# LATE THINKER

Remembering mountain farms
that gleam far for lost men,
he knows by sympathy
tonight by the steady stove,
questioning one grain at a time,
wandering like a dune,
easy with the wind—
that some kind of organization
is the right way to live.

A secret friend of those lands
where certain plants hide in the woods,
he stands with them. In the fern
he shoulders pack. In the dark
he joins the star-striding men
who crossed the continent
following, toward the low sky,
ocean-generous clouds
to the firred mountains of Oregon

Or maybe—tie, rail, spike—
to hay towns beyond Salt Lake:
store fronts winds have tasted,
paint that summers tested—
he questions those pale towns,
turns to those haggard lands.
Where are the wrongs men have done?
He holds out calloused hands
toward that landscape of justice.

He counts each daily meeting
the stare of its blind meaning,
and maintains an autumn allegiance,
but what can he lean toward?
Remembering the wild places, bitter,
where pale fields meet winter,
he searches for some right song
that could catch and then shake the world,
any night by the steady stove.

# A LOOK RETURNED

At the border of October
where Montana meets Alberta
that white grass that worshipped wind
climbed from summer to the sky,
which began to change.

I saw that day that day relate
winter's province to the state,
and clouds correct the fence's stance
where a hill twisted the line
of the seamless land.

All countries have their majesties
and meet October in various ways,
harking toward wonder every winter,
trying again for their best picture
at their best times;

But that state so north it curled behind
the map in hands of snow and wind,
clutching the end of no place—
I hold that state before my face,
and learn my life.

## INTERLUDE

Think of a river beyond your thought
avoiding your sight by being so pure
that it can turn anywhere any rock says
but always be ready for the next real call,
and beyond such a river this ritual night
think of summer weather questioning the corn
contoured for rain, while the lightning crawls,
and a face like a news event approaches the world.

Then come back in our cave of space
and wait for the wonder of that face.

# In Dear Detail, by Ideal Light

### I

Night huddled our town,
plunged from the sky.
You moved away.
I save what I can of the time.

In other towns, calling my name,
home people hale me, dazed;
those moments we hold,
reciting in the evening,

Reciting about you, receding
through the huddle of any new town.
Can we rescue the light
that happened, and keeps on happening, around us?

Gradually we left you there
surrounded by the river curve
and the held-out arms,
elms under the streetlight.

These vision emergencies come
wherever we go—
blind home
coming near at unlikely places.

2

One's duty: to find a place
that grows from his part of the world—
it means leaving
certain good people.

Think: near High Trail, Colorado,
a wire follows cottonwoods
helping one to know—
like a way on trust.

That lonely strand leaves the road
depending on limbs or little poles,
and slants away,
hunting a ranch in the hills.

There, for the rest of the years,
by not going there, a person could believe
some porch looking south,
and steady in the shade—maybe you,

Rescued by how the hills
happened to arrive where they are,
depending on that wire
going to an imagined place
Where finally the way the world feels
really means how things are,
in dear detail,
by ideal light all around us.

# THE WANDERER AWAITING PREFERMENT

In a world where no one knows for sure
I hold the blanket for the snow to find:
*come winter, then the blizzard, then demand—*
*the final strategy of right, the snow*
*like justice over stones like bread.*

"Tell us what you deserve," the whole world said.
My hands belong to cold; my voice to dust,
nobody's brother; and with a gray-eyed stare
the towns I pass return me what I give, or claim:
"Wanderer, swerve: but this is a faint command."

Only what winter gives, I claim. As trees
drink dark through roots for their peculiar grain
while meager justice applauds up through the grass,
I calm the private storm within myself.
Men should not claim, nor should they have to ask.

# VOCATION

This dream the world is having about itself
includes a trace on the plains of the Oregon trail,
a groove in the grass my father showed us all
one day while meadowlarks were trying to tell
something better about to happen.

I dreamed the trace to the mountains, over the hills,
and there a girl who belonged wherever she was.
But then my mother called us back to the car:
she was afraid; she always blamed the place,
the time, anything my father planned.

Now both of my parents, the long line through the plain,
the meadowlarks, the sky, the world's whole dream
remain, and I hear him say while I stand between the two,
helpless, both of them part of me:
"Your job is to find what the world is trying to be."

# AFTERWORD

AT THE MOMENT OF WRITING, when one of those fortunate strokes of composition takes place, the poet does sometimes feel that he is accomplishing an exhilarating, a wonderful, a stupendous job; he glimpses at such times how it might be to overwhelm the universe by rightness, to do something peculiarly difficult to such a perfect pitch that something like a revelation comes. For that instant, conceiving is knowing; the secret life in language reveals the very self of things.

It is awkward for the poet in our time to own up to such a grandiose feeling, and the feeling may not last long, nor make much lasting impression. But it is at the heart of the chore of creating. We may remember mostly the long stupid look at the material before us, and then maybe a kind of slow, emotional thinking. That is a lonely-helpless feeling. At the time, the writer is responsible for everything, and at the same time he is simply lost. He has to be willing to stay lost until what he finds—or what finds him—has the validity that the instant (with him as its sole representative) can recognize. At that moment he is transported, not because he wants to be but because he can't help it. Out of the wilderness of possibility comes a vine without a name, and his poem is growing with it.

*From William Stafford's remarks on receiving the National Book Award for* Traveling Through the Dark *in New York City, March 12, 1963.*

other contemporary american poetry
available from **weatherlight**

Robert Bly
WHAT HAVE I EVER LOST BY DYING?
*Collected Prose Poems*
ISBN 0-9522798-0-0. £6.99

William Stafford
HOLDING ONTO THE GRASS
ISBN 0-9522798-1-9. £6.99

Robert Bly
MEDITATIONS ON THE INSATIABLE SOUL
ISBN 0-9522798-2-7 £6.99

Orders with 10% postage to
Windhorse Publications
11 Park Road
Moseley
Birmingham B13 8AB
England
Tel/Fax: 0121 449 9191
E-Mail: 100331.3327
@compuserve.com